Reinhard Gehlen's Double Life

Gehlen's Journey from Nazi to CIA

Eleanor T. Whitfield

Copyright © Eleanor T. Whitfield, 2024.

All rights reserved.

Thankful to you for consenting to protected innovation guidelines by downloading this book through genuine methods and by not replicating, checking, or spreading any piece of this book.

Table of Contents

Introduction

Chapter 1: The Rise of an Intelligence Officer

Chapter 2: World War II: The Eastern Front

Chapter 3: Crafting the Wehrmacht's Intelligence Network

Chapter 4: The Fall of the Third Reich

Chapter 5: Negotiating with the Americans

Chapter 6: Operation Paperclip and Integration into the CIA

Chapter 7: Cold War Operative

Chapter 8: Espionage in the Cold War

Chapter 9: Controversies and Criticisms

Chapter 10: Retirement and Memoirs

Conclusion

Introduction

Reinhard Gehlen remains one of the most interesting and controversial personalities in the history of espionage. His dual positions throughout World War II and the following Cold War depict a career distinguished by tremendous impact and complicated allegiances. This introduction digs into an overview of Gehlen's dual positions and the tremendous importance of his espionage actions.

During World War II, Gehlen served as Hitler's chief intelligence officer on the Eastern Front. As the chief of the Foreign Armies East (Fremde Heere Ost, FHO), Gehlen was responsible for obtaining and evaluating information on the Soviet Union. His study was vital to the Wehrmacht's operations, offering strategic insights regarding Soviet military capabilities and movements. Despite the final defeat of Nazi Germany, Gehlen's competence and the massive intelligence network he had established did not go unnoticed by the Allies.

After the war, expecting the fall of the Third Reich, Gehlen made a strategic choice to retain his intelligence files and give his services to the United States. This action was inspired by his prediction of the approaching battle between the Western Allies and the Soviet Union. Gehlen's surrender to American troops signaled the beginning of his second career as a vital intelligence asset for the United States.

In the early years of the Cold War, Gehlen was key in forming the Gehlen Organization, which ultimately became the Bundesnachrichtendienst

(BND), West Germany's federal intelligence organization. His function transformed from a Nazi espionage officer to a critical ally in the battle against communism. Under the aegis of the CIA, Gehlen's outfit became the premier intelligence agency in West Germany, focused on espionage efforts against the Soviet Union and Eastern Bloc nations.

Gehlen's espionage actions had far-reaching ramifications for both World War II and the Cold War. During the war, his intelligence efforts on the Eastern Front gave the German military with important information regarding Soviet troop movements, strengths, and strategy.

His network of spies and informants inside the Soviet Union was substantial, and his analytical reports were highly regarded by the German

High Command. Despite the final defeat of Nazi Germany, Gehlen's intelligence activities slowed Soviet advances on multiple fronts, illustrating the importance of his work.

The journey from a Nazi intelligence officer to a significant role in American and West German intelligence circles is possibly the most astonishing part of Gehlen's career. His choice to engage with the United States was influenced by pragmatic factors and a deep-seated anti-communism.

The Gehlen Organization, manned mostly by former Nazi intelligence operatives, became a vital weapon for the CIA in its attempts to oppose Soviet influence in Europe.

Gehlen's impact in the Cold War period cannot be overestimated. His group supplied the United States with crucial information about Soviet military capabilities and intentions. The intelligence obtained by Gehlen's network was vital in formulating American and NATO tactics during the early years of the Cold War.

Moreover, the foundation of the BND under Gehlen's supervision assured that West Germany had a formidable intelligence infrastructure that could act independently while keeping close relations with Western intelligence services.

However, Gehlen's legacy is not without dispute. His recruiting of former Nazis into the Gehlen Organization and the BND has been a source of substantial criticism. Critics believe that this weakened the moral integrity of the post-war

German intelligence agency and enabled persons with dubious pasts to hold enormous authority. Despite these difficulties, Gehlen's contributions to the field of espionage and his effect on Cold War dynamics remain undisputed.

Chapter 1: The Rise of an Intelligence Officer

Reinhard Gehlen's early years and his path into the military are important to understanding his growth into one of the most intriguing and prominent intelligence officers of the 20th century. This chapter dives into his background, the forces that formed his goals, and his early military career, laying the tone for his subsequent prominence in both Nazi Germany and the Cold War espionage environment.

Gehlen's Upbringing and Entry into the Military

Reinhard Gehlen was born on April 3, 1902, in Erfurt, a city in central Germany. He was the oldest of three boys in a middle-class household.

His father, a bookstore, instilled in him a desire for information and discipline, while his mother created a loving and supportive atmosphere. The qualities of hard effort, intellectual curiosity, and resilience were implanted in Gehlen from an early age, determining his future course.

As a young lad, Gehlen exhibited a deep interest in history and geography, topics that would later prove important in his intelligence work. He was a dedicated student, recognized for his analytical intellect and attention to detail. These attributes, along with his patriotic passion, encouraged him to seek a military career, inspired by the stories of valor and strategy he read in literature and heard from soldiers of World War I.

In 1920, at the age of 18, Gehlen entered the Reichswehr, the military organization of the

Weimar Republic, which was restricted to 100,000 personnel by the Treaty of Versailles. Despite the limits, the Reichswehr was a professional and well-disciplined organization, offering a good training ground for future military commanders.

Gehlen's choice to join the military was not simply a reflection of his ambition but also a reaction to the unstable political and economic environment of post-war Germany.

Initial Postings and Rise Through the Ranks
Gehlen's early years in the Reichswehr were defined by intensive training and an emphasis on creating a foundation in military tactics and leadership. He attended the Infantry School in Dresden, where he excelled in his studies and exhibited a natural knack for strategic thinking.

His professors recognized his ability to stay cool under pressure and his capacity for processing complicated knowledge quickly—skills that would eventually characterize his career in intelligence.

After graduating from the Infantry School, Gehlen obtained his first assignment as a junior officer in a unit stationed in Bavaria. Here, he received real experience in directing soldiers and improved his talents in logistics and operations management. His superiors were pleased by his performance, and he rapidly gained a reputation as a professional and loyal officer.

Gehlen's early career coincided with a moment of major political turmoil in Germany. The advent of the Nazi Party and Adolf Hitler's accession to power in 1933 brought about profound changes in the military. The Reichswehr was rebuilt and enlarged into the Wehrmacht, and Gehlen, like many of his colleagues, had to manage the new political situation cautiously. While he was not an enthusiastic admirer of the Nazi philosophy, he saw the need of associating himself with the dictatorship to progress his career.

In 1935, Gehlen was chosen to attend the famous Kriegsakademie (War Academy) in Berlin, an institution responsible for preparing the future commanders of the German military.

Admission to the Kriegsakademie was exceedingly difficult, and Gehlen's selection was a testimonial to his aptitude. The curriculum at the school was broad, including advanced military strategy, geopolitics, and intelligence.

Gehlen's performance at the school was exceptional, garnering him the admiration of his classmates and professors alike.

Upon graduation from the Kriegsakademie, Gehlen was advanced to the rank of captain and sent to the General Staff, the elite organization responsible for planning and executing Germany's military operations. This position constituted a key turning point in his career, as it provided him with a chance to work with some of the most powerful persons in the Wehrmacht. It was here that Gehlen's interest in intelligence started to take form.

Gehlen's first significant post on the General Staff was in the Operations Division, where he was engaged in the planning of Germany's rearmament and the execution of new military concepts. His thorough approach to preparing and his ability to predict future obstacles got him commendations from his superiors. During this period, he also started to build a network of connections inside the intelligence community, realizing the important role that information and espionage would play in future wars.

In 1939, as Europe teetered on the verge of war, Gehlen was elevated to the rank of major and posted to the Foreign Armies East (Fremde Heere Ost, or FHO) branch of the General Staff.

The FHO was charged with obtaining and interpreting information about the Soviet Union, which was considered Germany's principal foe in the east. This task was a perfect match for Gehlen, given his analytical talents and profound awareness of Eastern Europe's topography and political scene.

Under the direction of General Franz Halder, the Chief of the General Staff, the FHO became a crucial component of Germany's intelligence infrastructure.

Gehlen's function in the FHO involves managing the collection of information from numerous sources, including reconnaissance units, spies, and seized enemy papers. He soon exhibited an ability to combine different bits of information into clear and useful intelligence reports.

One of Gehlen's most noteworthy achievements during this time was his work on the planning for Operation Barbarossa, the German invasion of the Soviet Union in 1941. He played a vital role in analyzing the size and placement of Soviet troops, as well as detecting possible flaws in the Soviet command system. His findings gave vital information that informed the planning and execution of the invasion.

Gehlen's accomplishment in the FHO did not go unnoticed. In 1942, he was promoted to lieutenant colonel and named Chief of Intelligence for the Eastern Front, reporting directly to Heinz Guderian, one of Germany's most senior military commanders. This role placed Gehlen at the vanguard of Germany's intelligence activities against the Soviet Union, confirming his reputation as a master of military intelligence.

As Chief of Intelligence, Gehlen was responsible for directing a huge network of intelligence agents and analysts. He established novel procedures for obtaining and evaluating intelligence, including the use of aerial surveillance, intercepted communications, and prisoner interrogations. His work contributed to numerous crucial intelligence discoveries, including the discovery of Soviet military movements and supply routes.

Despite the hurdles created by the hard circumstances of the Eastern Front and the powerful Soviet espionage measures, Gehlen's work proved crucial to the German war effort. His ability to foresee Soviet strategy and tactics helped the Wehrmacht to score numerous important successes, but the tide of the war would finally shift against Germany.

By the conclusion of World War II, Gehlen had risen to the rank of colonel and was generally recognized as one of Germany's best intelligence operatives. His experiences on the Eastern Front and his contributions to the German military's intelligence skills provided the framework for his post-war career. As the war concluded, Gehlen started to evaluate his future and the various chances that may emerge in the quickly shifting geopolitical scene.

Gehlen's early years and military goals, distinguished by a mix of rigorous training, strategic brilliance, and a clear appreciation of the value of intelligence, laid the foundation for his metamorphosis into a pivotal player in the Cold War.

His capacity to adapt and succeed in the complicated and sometimes dangerous world of military espionage would define his career and leave an everlasting effect on the history of intelligence operations.

Chapter 2: World War II: The Eastern Front

Reinhard Gehlen's appointment as Chief of Intelligence under General Heinz Guderian was a key period in his military career and the larger extent of World War II espionage. In 1942, as the war raged on the Eastern Front, Gehlen was picked for his analytical talents and ability to integrate complicated material into useful intelligence.

Guderian, a notable military strategist recognized for his formulation of blitzkrieg tactics, wanted an intelligence officer who could match his strategic vision and operational objectives.

Gehlen's mission was to supervise the collection and analysis of information about the Soviet Union's military capabilities and movements. His position occurred at a time when accurate and timely information was critical for the success of German operations in the wide and frequently unpredictable Eastern Front.

Gehlen's ability to deliver precise assessments and projections gained him Guderian's confidence, and he swiftly became a vital member of the German High Command's strategic planning.

Key Operations and Intelligence Strategies
Gehlen's term as Chief of Intelligence entailed numerous major operations and the adoption of advanced intelligence methods. One of his key duties was to develop a formidable intelligence

network capable of penetrating the Soviet Union's carefully guarded military establishment. To do this, Gehlen focused on several crucial areas:

Human Intelligence (HUMINT): Gehlen put substantial emphasis on human intelligence, recruiting and supervising a network of spies and informants inside the Soviet lands. These informants supplied firsthand details of troop movements, military sites, and strategic plans.

Gehlen's network comprised dissatisfied Soviet officers, local collaborators, and prisoners of war who were eager to offer intelligence in return for their protection.

Signal Intelligence (SIGINT): Recognizing the need for intercepting and decoding Soviet communications, Gehlen extended the use of signal intelligence. His team worked relentlessly to crack Soviet codes and ciphers, giving crucial insights into enemy plans and actions. The intelligence gathered by SIGINT was vital in forecasting Soviet offensives and reacting efficiently.

Aerial Reconnaissance: Gehlen's intelligence operations also depended significantly on aerial reconnaissance. He oversaw sorties that obtained high-resolution images of Soviet locations, which were subsequently evaluated to determine troop concentrations, supply depots, and defensive buildings. This visual information supplemented the data obtained from other sources, offering a holistic picture of the battlefield.

Prisoner Interrogations: Interrogating captured Soviet troops was another crucial aspect of Gehlen's approach. His team devised innovative questioning tactics to get vital information from inmates. The data collected from these meetings frequently revealed the Soviet order of battle, strategic aims, and logistical shortcomings.

Challenges and Successes on the Eastern Front

Operating on the Eastern Front faced Gehlen with significant obstacles, both logistical and strategic. The enormous expanse of the Soviet Union, along with its severe climate and rugged terrain, made information collection a daunting undertaking. Additionally, the Soviet military's secrecy and counterintelligence procedures faced considerable difficulties in acquiring credible information.

Logistical Challenges: The immense distances involved in the Eastern Front operations demanded substantial logistical preparation. Maintaining communication links, providing operatives in the field, and guaranteeing the timely delivery of intelligence reports were ongoing issues. Gehlen's network had to function over thousands of kilometers, frequently in dangerous locations where supply lines were pushed thin.

Soviet Counterintelligence: The Soviet Union's NKVD (the forerunner to the KGB) was a strong opponent in the domain of counterintelligence. The NKVD aggressively attempted to locate and eliminate German spies and informants. Gehlen's operatives faced the continual prospect of arrest and death, making their job exceptionally risky. Despite these hazards, Gehlen's network managed to enter crucial regions and acquire vital intelligence.

Operational victories: Despite the hurdles, Gehlen's intelligence operations generated considerable victories that had a profound influence on the war effort. One major success was the correct forecast of Soviet counteroffensives during the Battle of Kursk in 1943.

Gehlen's analysis of troop movements and intercepted communications helped the German High Command to plan fortifications that impeded the Soviet assault, but it ultimately did not influence the result of the fight.

Strategic Impact: Gehlen's intelligence inputs were crucial in numerous other significant missions. His assessments of the Soviet buildup in the Caucasus area in 1942 impacted German plans during the Battle of Stalingrad. Although the fight resulted in a terrible loss for Germany, Gehlen's intelligence gave critical insights into Soviet capabilities and intentions, impacting the strategic choices of the German leadership.

Long-Term Influence: Gehlen's work on the Eastern Front also had long-term repercussions for post-war intelligence operations. The procedures and networks he built were subsequently merged into the Gehlen Organization, which formed the core of West Germany's Federal Intelligence Service (BND). His experiences on the Eastern Front impacted his attitude toward Cold War espionage, making him a significant player in the intelligence establishment for decades.

Reinhard Gehlen's appointment as Heinz Guderian's Chief of Intelligence and his subsequent actions on the Eastern Front reflect a complicated and significant chapter in the history of World War II espionage. His ability to handle the great hurdles of obtaining and interpreting information in one of the most hostile circumstances of the war revealed his outstanding talents and strategic insight.

The triumphs and defeats he encountered not only altered the outcome of the war but also established the framework for his eventual involvement in establishing post-war intelligence operations throughout the Cold War.

Chapter 3: Crafting the Wehrmacht's Intelligence Network

Reinhard Gehlen, one of the most enigmatic figures in the history of espionage, played a pivotal role in crafting the Wehrmacht's intelligence network during World War II. His journey from a relatively obscure military officer to the chief architect of Nazi Germany's intelligence operations on the Eastern Front reveals the complexities and intricacies of wartime espionage.

This chapter goes into the construction and structure of the espionage systems under Gehlen's command, his cooperation with other intelligence groups, and the important intelligence achievements that marked his career.

Establishment and Organization of Espionage Systems

Reinhard Gehlen's participation in military intelligence started in earnest when he was appointed as the chief of the Foreign Armies East (Fremde Heere Ost or FHO) in 1942. This department was charged with obtaining and evaluating information about the Soviet Union, an essential responsibility as the Wehrmacht prepared for and fought in the titanic war on the Eastern Front.

Gehlen realized early on the significance of a systematic and rigorous approach to information collection. He concentrated on five critical aspects to develop a successful espionage system:

Recruitment and Training: Gehlen favored the recruitment of personnel with language skills, geographical expertise, and a profound grasp of Soviet military philosophy. He also devised intensive training programs to guarantee that his operators were well-versed in espionage methods, cryptography, and data analysis.

Network Establishment: Under Gehlen's guidance, the FHO built a huge network of operatives and informants behind enemy lines. This network comprised German troops who had defected, anti-communist townspeople and prisoners of war prepared to cooperate. Gehlen's spies worked in hostile territory, acquiring important intelligence on Soviet army movements, supplies, and strategic intentions.

Signal Intelligence (SIGINT): Gehlen put substantial emphasis on SIGINT, believing that intercepting and decoding Soviet communications would give priceless insights. He coordinated operations with the Wehrmacht's signal intelligence divisions, strengthening the ability of the FHO to monitor and decipher enemy broadcasts.

Human Intelligence (HUMINT): Gehlen's HUMINT operations were vast and featured deep-cover operatives implanted inside Soviet-controlled territories. These spies obtained firsthand intelligence on Soviet military capabilities, political events, and the morale of both soldiers and citizens.

Analytical Rigor: Gehlen developed a culture of analytical rigor inside the FHO. He underlined the need for cross-referencing intelligence from numerous sources and validating results to minimize misrepresentation. Detailed reports and strategic evaluations were often written and given to high-ranking officers in the Wehrmacht and the Nazi leadership.

Gehlen's organizational skills and strategic vision developed the FHO into a powerful intelligence operation. His efforts in developing a comprehensive espionage infrastructure would subsequently be important not just during the war but also in his post-war career with the Americans.

Collaboration with Other Intelligence Units

Collaboration was a cornerstone of Gehlen's approach to intelligence. He knew that successful espionage needed collaboration with other intelligence groups inside the German military and outside. His ability to form coalitions and combine disparate intelligence activities was key to the success of the FHO.

Wehrmacht Intelligence Units: Gehlen worked closely with numerous intelligence departments inside the Wehrmacht. He maintained excellent links with the Abwehr (military intelligence agency) and the Sicherheitsdienst (SD), the intelligence wing of the SS. This cooperation permitted the exchange of crucial information and resources, strengthening the overall intelligence capabilities of the German military.

International Intelligence agencies: Gehlen also cultivated ties with international intelligence agencies, notably those of Germany's allies. Notably, he coordinated with the intelligence services of Finland, Hungary, and Romania, which gave important information on Soviet military activity in their respective territories. These relationships broadened the breadth of Gehlen's network and enriched the intelligence pool accessible to the FHO.

Technical Intelligence Collaboration: In the domain of technical intelligence, Gehlen coordinated operations with the German cryptography outfit known as the B-Dienst. This squad specialized in cracking Soviet codes and ciphers. By merging the work of B-Dienst with his activities, Gehlen maintained a continual supply of encrypted communications that revealed important insights into Soviet strategy and movements.

Field Operations Coordination: Gehlen's FHO forces regularly coordinated directly with frontline Wehrmacht troops. This tight synchronization allowed for real-time information exchange, which was vital during large military operations. For example, during the Battle of Kursk, Gehlen's information about Soviet fortifications and counteroffensive preparations was essential in influencing German operations.

Scientific and technological Intelligence: Gehlen recognized the value of scientific and technological intelligence in knowing the capabilities of the Soviet war machine. He engaged with professionals in numerous sectors, including engineers, scientists, and intellectuals, to examine Soviet technology and armament. This interdisciplinary approach improved the information generated by the FHO and gave the Wehrmacht with a more thorough picture of their foe.

Major Intelligence Breakthroughs

Gehlen's careful methodology and joint efforts resulted in numerous big intelligence discoveries that had enormous implications on the Eastern Front and beyond. These achievements not only revealed the efficacy of his espionage network but also emphasized the strategic usefulness of intelligence in battle.

Operation Barbarossa Preparations: One of Gehlen's early triumphs was his participation in the preparation of Operation Barbarossa, the

German invasion of the Soviet Union. His knowledge of Soviet force formations and logistics was vital in determining the early assault preparations. While the operation eventually encountered severe obstacles, the early stages benefitted from Gehlen's observations.

Battle of Stalingrad: During the Battle of Stalingrad, Gehlen's intelligence network gave precise updates on Soviet reinforcements and supply routes. Despite the final German loss, Gehlen's research enabled the Wehrmacht to predict Soviet counteroffensives and make tactical modifications in the hard urban combat environment.

Soviet Winter Offensive of 1942-1943: Gehlen's insight in forecasting the Soviet Winter

Offensive of 1942-1943 enabled the German high command to plan defensive measures that minimized some of the repercussions of the Soviet assault. His precise estimates of Soviet strength and movements were important in building defense strategies.

Operation Bagration: One of the most notable intelligence achievements under Gehlen's command was the prediction of Operation Bagration, the huge Soviet summer attack in 1944. Gehlen's network offered early warnings about the scope and intentions of the attack, allowing the Wehrmacht to reinforce vital regions and avert even worse casualties.

Post-War Legacy: The intelligence breakthroughs gained by Gehlen's network had a lasting influence after the war. The information and procedures produced under his supervision were crucial in the development of West Germany's intelligence agency, the Bundesnachrichtendienst (BND), during the Cold War. Gehlen's ability to switch from serving Nazi Germany to becoming a significant asset for the United States and its allies underlined the lasting worth of his intelligence skills.

Chapter 4: The Fall of the Third Reich

Reinhard Gehlen, one of Hitler's senior intelligence officials on the Eastern Front, observed the downfall of the Third Reich personally. As the war came to a conclusion in early 1945, Gehlen and his team confronted the difficult job of conducting intelligence activities amidst the turmoil and fall of Nazi Germany.

Gehlen was fully aware that the end was approaching. The Allied troops were closing in from the west, while the Soviets moved mercilessly from the east. As Hitler's government disintegrated, Gehlen had to plan forward, not just for his safety but also for the massive quantity of information his team had accumulated over the years.

During these stormy last days, Gehlen's headquarters, the Foreign Armies East (Fremde Heere Ost), was situated in the highlands of Bavaria. The outfit had been charged with collecting intelligence on the Soviet Union and had gathered a lot of knowledge about the Red Army's movements, capabilities, and vulnerabilities.

This knowledge was essential, not only for the Germans but possibly for the Allies in the post-war era. Gehlen knew that this knowledge may be his ticket to survival and future importance.

As the situation worsened, Gehlen planned a strategy to retain his intelligence assets. He and his loyal aides microfilmed vital papers and hid them in impermeable drums, which were subsequently buried in different sites in the Bavarian Alps.

This operation was a deliberate maneuver, intended at preserving important information that may subsequently be utilized as leverage with the Allies. The choice to conceal these records shows Gehlen's foresight and his appreciation of the strategic worth of the material in his hands.

Gehlen's last days in the Nazi government were characterized by a delicate balancing act. On one side, he had to preserve his function within the Wehrmacht and avoid provoking suspicion. On the other side, he was planning for a future when Nazi Germany no longer existed. This dual emphasis needed a high degree of cleverness and a precise awareness of the continuously shifting geopolitical scene.

Capturing and Preserving Intelligence Assets
The retention of intelligence assets was a vital part of Gehlen's policy as the Third Reich crumbled. The papers buried in the Bavarian Alps provided precise information on Soviet military strategy, troop deployments, and infrastructure.

Gehlen recognized that this knowledge would be essential to the Allies, notably the Americans, who were gearing up for a lengthy battle with the Soviet Union, which subsequently became the Cold War.

Gehlen's choice to microfilm the papers ensured that the intelligence could be readily transferred and disguised. The waterproof drums offered protection against the elements, ensuring that the information would stay intact for future use. This thorough approach emphasized Gehlen's appreciation of the value of his work and his determination to protect it at all costs.

In addition to preserving physical documents, Gehlen also took steps to secure his most valuable asset: his team. The men under his command were seasoned intelligence officers with extensive knowledge of Soviet military operations. Gehlen realized that their knowledge would be just as useful to the Allies as the materials they had concealed. He devised measures to guarantee that his essential troops might elude arrest by the Soviets and reach the American lines, where they could give their services to the Allies.

The collapse of the Third Reich saw many high-ranking Nazi leaders seeking to leave or go into hiding. Gehlen, however, took a different course. Rather than simply trying to escape, he positioned himself and his team as valuable assets to the incoming Allied forces.

This strategy required careful planning and execution. Gehlen had to ensure that his men could navigate the chaotic and dangerous environment of a collapsing Germany while maintaining the integrity of their intelligence. Gehlen's efforts to preserve intelligence assets also involved a significant degree of risk. If the Soviets had discovered the hidden documents or captured his team, the consequences would have been dire. Gehlen himself faced the constant threat of arrest or execution by both the remaining Nazi authorities and the advancing Soviet forces. His ability to handle these dangers and effectively execute his strategy emphasized his talent as an intelligence officer and his commitment to ensuring a future for himself and his soldiers.

Initial Contact with the Allies

As the Third Reich crumbled, Gehlen made the critical decision to surrender to the Americans rather than the Soviets. He assumed that the Americans would be more receptive to his offer of information and may provide safety for him and his crew. This decision was based on his assessment of the emerging geopolitical landscape, where the United States and the

Soviet Union were poised to become the dominant superpowers in a post-war world.

Gehlen's initial contact with the Americans was a carefully orchestrated operation. In early May 1945, Hitler and a small number of his closest aides made their way to the American lines, bringing with them a sample of the microfilmed papers. Gehlen presented himself to the Americans not as a defeated Nazi officer, but as a valuable intelligence asset with critical information on the Soviet Union.

Gehlen's attitude was realistic and businesslike. He underlined the strategic worth of his information and the skill of his team, giving them to the Americans in return for security and the ability to continue their job. The Americans, seeing the potential advantages of Gehlen's suggestion, were first apprehensive but intrigued. The timing of Gehlen's suggestion was serendipitous, as the American intelligence community was already pondering ways to obtain information on the Soviet Union, their former friend turned prospective opponent.

Gehlen's negotiations with the Americans were conducted under the supervision of the Office of Strategic Services (OSS), the precursor to the CIA. The OSS officers were impressed by the depth and quality of the intelligence Gehlen presented.

They recognized the importance of his knowledge of Soviet military capabilities and his network of informants and connections. Gehlen's plan to create a new intelligence outfit that could function under American supervision was considered a plausible answer to their need for dependable information on the Soviets.

The official agreement between Gehlen and the Americans signified the beginning of a new era in his career. The Americans enabled the rescue of the buried intelligence materials and provided safety for Gehlen and his crew. In exchange, Gehlen and his troops were absorbed into the American intelligence system, setting the framework for what would eventually become the Gehlen Organization.

This first interaction with the Allies was a turning moment for Gehlen. It enabled him to move from a high-ranking official in a defeated state to a prominent actor in the burgeoning Cold War intelligence battlefield. His ability to adapt to the fast-changing conditions and position himself as an important asset to the Americans saved his life and laid the groundwork for his future services to Western intelligence activities.

Chapter 5: Negotiating with the Americans

As World War II came to a conclusion, Reinhard Gehlen, cognizant of the oncoming fall of Nazi Germany, found himself at a crucial point. His deep knowledge of the Soviet Union, obtained as the commander of Fremde Heere Ost (FHO), the Wehrmacht's military intelligence division on the Eastern Front, made him a vital asset. Gehlen sought to utilize this information in a determined fight for survival and significance in the post-war world.

Gehlen painstakingly arranged his surrender. Understanding that the Allies, notably the Americans, would greatly appreciate his information on the Soviet Union, he guaranteed the preservation of important papers. In early May 1945, when the Third Reich disintegrated, Gehlen and a limited number of his loyal officers hid microfilms and papers in weatherproof steel barrels in the Bavarian Alps. These provided extensive intelligence reports on Soviet military capabilities, plans, and political insights.

On May 22, 1945, Gehlen surrendered to the U.S. Army Counterintelligence Corps (CIC) in the hamlet of Fischhausen in Bavaria. Unlike many of his predecessors, Gehlen was not in full military uniform but wore civilian clothing, a conscious gesture to disassociate himself from the Nazi government. His first move upon surrendering was to provide his intelligence files on the Soviet Union as a negotiating chip.

Gehlen's original kidnappers, seeing the potential worth of his knowledge, immediately escalated his case. He was assigned to the Seventh Army's intelligence headquarters in Augsburg, where his idea was considered seriously.

Gehlen, ever the savvy negotiator, underlined the strategic benefit his information might bring to the United States, particularly as tensions with the Soviet Union were already starting to rise.

Initial Assessments and Negotiations

The Americans were first wary about Gehlen's offer. To them, he was a high-ranking Nazi official, and his sudden desire to help was viewed with mistrust. However, early reviews of the materials he submitted indicated their great importance. The precise data on Soviet troop deployments, orders of battle, and military strategy were unlike anything the Americans possessed. This first appraisal established the scene for further formal talks.

Gehlen was questioned extensively. His grasp of the Soviet military and political system pleased his American interrogators, who concluded that this information may be significant in the evolving geopolitical scene. Gehlen, mindful of the mistrust around him, was forthright about his objectives. He contended that his skills might assist the United States defeat the Soviet threat, which he considered a mutual adversary.

High-level leaders in the U.S. military and intelligence establishment, notably General Edwin Sibert, Assistant Chief of Staff for Intelligence in the U.S. Army, took an interest in

Gehlen. Sibert and others recognized the promise of exploiting Gehlen's network to collect information on the Soviet Union, which was swiftly becoming the new opponent in the burgeoning Cold War. The Americans understood that Gehlen's existing network of connections and agents inside the Soviet area of influence may be beneficial.

Negotiations were tricky. Gehlen wanted guarantees for himself and his soldiers, including immunity from prosecution for war crimes and pledges for their safety. He also wanted to guarantee that his company would stay intact and operating. The Americans, knowing the strategic value of Gehlen's network, agreed to these stipulations. In exchange, Gehlen offered complete cooperation and the resurrection of his intelligence organization, this time for American interests.

The agreement was finalized during the summer of 1945. Gehlen and a core group of his officers were taken to the United States, where they were further debriefed and vetted. This phase was critical, as it enabled American intelligence to evaluate the authenticity and trustworthiness of Gehlen's information and to decide how best to incorporate his network into their own operations.

Transfer to American Custody

The handover of Gehlen and his staff to American captivity represented a turning point in post-war intelligence activities. Gehlen was first imprisoned at Fort Hunt, Virginia, a covert interrogation camp for high-value inmates.

During his tenure at Fort Hunt, Gehlen was exposed to comprehensive debriefing sessions, during which he offered detailed reports of his activities, his network, and the information he had obtained on the Soviet Union.

The Americans were pleased with Gehlen's professionalism and breadth of knowledge. His abilities to convey the complexity of Soviet military operations and his insights into Soviet political moves were unrivaled. This persuaded the U.S. intelligence community of the benefits of incorporating Gehlen and his network into their operations.

Gehlen's group, officially dubbed the Gehlen group (Org), was founded under American direction but functioned mostly independently. This autonomy was a prerequisite Gehlen insisted upon, thinking that only a well-coordinated, autonomous organization could properly acquire and evaluate information on the Soviet Union. The Org was transported back to Germany, where it functioned from the American occupation zone.

One of the key problems throughout the transfer was assuring the loyalty and trustworthiness of Gehlen's soldiers. The Americans wanted to be convinced that these former Nazi intelligence officials would not compromise their activities or had contradictory loyalties.

Rigorous screening methods were developed to filter out those who could represent a danger. This includes background checks, psychiatric tests, and regular surveillance.

The Gehlen Organization immediately became a key tool for the Americans. It provided a steady stream of intelligence on Soviet military capabilities and movements, as well as political developments within the Eastern Bloc. This knowledge was vital throughout the early years of the Cold War, helping to determine U.S. foreign policy and military strategy.

Gehlen's collaboration with the Americans was not without criticism. Many within the U.S. and allied governments were apprehensive about dealing with former high-ranking Nazis.

Critics stated that this relationship violated moral and ethical norms. However, the geopolitical imperatives of the Cold War sometimes overshadowed these concerns. The pressing necessity for reliable and actionable information on the Soviet Union took priority, and Gehlen's group produced results.

In 1949, the Gehlen Organization was officially merged into the newly founded West German intelligence organization, the Bundesnachrichtendienst (BND), with Gehlen as its first president. This action established Gehlen's status as a crucial player in Cold War intelligence, bridging the gap between the destroyed Third Reich and the rising Federal Republic of Germany.

Chapter 6: Operation Paperclip and Integration into the CIA

Operation Paperclip was a secret initiative started by the United States after the close of World War II, aiming at recruiting German scientists, engineers, and intelligence agents to strengthen American experience and capabilities during the nascent Cold War.

Reinhard Gehlen, who had been Hitler's chief intelligence officer on the Eastern Front, was a strong option for this operation owing to his vast understanding of Soviet military tactics and his established network of intelligence assets.

Gehlen's first encounter with the Americans happened just before the fall of Nazi Germany. Anticipating loss, Gehlen took precautions to preserve his own life and possibly future value.

He had his huge intelligence files microfilmed and buried in the Bavarian Alps, saving important material that he felt would be beneficial to the Allies. In May 1945, Gehlen and a small handful of his loyal commanders surrendered to American troops, not as prisoners of war, but as prospective assets.

During his first debriefing, Gehlen made a strong case for his American prisoners. He believed that his skills and intelligence network were crucial for comprehending and fighting the Soviet threat. The Americans, seeing the significance of Gehlen's expertise and the opportunity to use his network, soon brought him to the United States for additional discussions. This marked the beginning of Gehlen's participation in Operation Paperclip.

Operation Paperclip was supposedly focused on scientific and technical professionals, but the participation of intelligence leaders like Gehlen highlighted the vast reach of the initiative. Gehlen's shift from a high-ranking Nazi official to a valued asset for the Americans was assisted by his pragmatic attitude and the urgency of the Cold War.

His desire to collaborate and the strategic value of his knowledge of the Soviet Union played a major factor in his admission and eventual integration into the US intelligence establishment.

Integration into the US Intelligence Community

Gehlen's incorporation into the US intelligence establishment was a complicated and diverse process. Initially, he and his close friends were kept in a secret facility at Fort Hunt, Virginia, where they underwent rigorous debriefing by American intelligence personnel.

During these discussions, Gehlen presented extensive information about Soviet military capabilities, plans, and people, proving the depth of his expertise and the importance of his intelligence network.

The Americans confronted a conundrum in their relations with Gehlen. On one side, his knowledge and intellect were important; on the other hand, there were enormous ethical and political problems about engaging a former high-ranking Nazi official. Despite these worries, the compelling need for dependable information on the Soviet Union outweighed the possible threats. Thus, Gehlen's promise to restart his network and supply continuing information was accepted.

Gehlen was repatriated to Germany in 1946 when he started the process of reconstructing his intelligence outfit under American direction. Initially operating under the codename "Operation Rusty," this endeavor entailed reestablishing touch with past agents and extending the network to include new recruits. The Americans supplied cash, logistical assistance, and political cover, enabling Gehlen to operate with a substantial degree of autonomy.

One of the important aspects of Gehlen's successful integration was his ability to adjust to the shifting political scene. He positioned himself not simply as a former Nazi commander but as a fervent anti-communist who could supply important information to the West.

This convergence with American strategic goals during the early Cold War era was essential in ensuring continuing backing and resources from the US.

Establishing the Gehlen Organization

The founding of the Gehlen Organization, sometimes known as the Gehlen Org, constituted a crucial milestone in the post-war intelligence scene. Officially founded in 1946, the group functioned as a semi-autonomous institution within the context of American intelligence activities in Germany. Its major objective was to acquire information on the Soviet Union and its Eastern Bloc allies, concentrating on military, political, and economic events.

The Gehlen Org operated out of a range of covert sites in West Germany. Its headquarters were first built in the little town of Pullach, near Munich. From this facility, Gehlen and his crew managed a wide network of spies and informants, leveraging both pre-existing connections from the war and fresh recruits recruited from varied backgrounds.

The group employed former Wehrmacht and SS officers, many of whom had substantial expertise in espionage and counterintelligence operations.

The Gehlen Org's efforts were wide-ranging and sophisticated. They included the interception and decryption of Soviet communications, the infiltration of Soviet and Eastern Bloc institutions, and the development of informants inside these governments.

The group also launched clandestine activities to weaken communist forces in Western Europe, so aligning its efforts with greater American and NATO policies.

One of the significant triumphs of the Gehlen Org was its capacity to offer timely and accurate information about Soviet military capabilities and intentions. This information was vital during critical Cold War crises, such as the Berlin Blockade and the Korean War, when knowledge of Soviet activities and intentions helped shape

Western reactions. The organization's achievements were acknowledged by American intelligence authorities, who continued to offer major assistance and cash.

Despite its triumphs, the Gehlen Org was not without criticism. The organization's hiring of former Nazis and war criminals generated condemnation, both inside the US and overseas. Moreover, there were continuous doubts about the credibility and allegiance of some of its operators, given their prior associations and possible ulterior intentions. These concerns were worsened by occasional operational failures and instances of corrupted intelligence.

In 1956, the Gehlen Org was formally integrated into the newly founded Bundesnachrichtendienst (BND), the Federal Intelligence Service of West

Germany. Gehlen was named as the first president of the BND, a post he maintained until his retirement in 1968. Under his direction, the BND maintained many of the actions launched by the Gehlen Org, retaining its emphasis on the Soviet Union and the Eastern Bloc.

Gehlen's shift from a Nazi intelligence officer to a significant role in the Cold War intelligence establishment was indicative of the larger complexity and moral ambiguities of the time.

His ability to exploit his skills and network to suit the geopolitical objectives of the West emphasized the pragmatic and sometimes merciless character of Cold War politics. While his legacy remains contentious, there is no doubting the substantial influence he had on the evolution of post-war intelligence operations and the larger Cold War battle between East and West.

Chapter 7: Cold War Operative

The founding of the Bundesnachrichtendienst (BND) was a crucial turning point in post-World War II intelligence operations and Cold War geopolitics. The BND was created in 1956, although its roots stretch back to the early post-war era when Reinhard Gehlen, a former high-ranking Nazi intelligence official, shifted from his involvement in the Third Reich to becoming a prominent actor in Western intelligence.

After World War II, Gehlen's network of intelligence assets, which had been important on the Eastern Front, was recognized as a significant resource by the U.S. intelligence establishment. Gehlen's great knowledge of Soviet military activities and his wide network of spies were viewed as important for the impending Cold War battle between the Western Allies and the Soviet Union.

This led to the founding of the Gehlen Organization, which functioned as an intelligence organization under American authority but ultimately provided the framework for Germany's intelligence activities.

In 1956, with the permission of Chancellor Konrad Adenauer and backing from U.S. authorities, the BND was formally founded. This approach was inspired by the imperative to develop a formidable intelligence operation that could successfully oppose Soviet influence and give strategic insights during the Cold War. The

BND was not just a symbol of Germany's reemergence as a sovereign state but also a realistic instrument in the Western intelligence armory against the Communist menace.

The BND was envisaged as a contemporary intelligence organization, aiming to promote West Germany's foreign policy and security aims while aligning with Western interests. Its establishment paralleled the larger geopolitical realities of the period when intelligence was a crucial aspect of national security and international diplomacy.

Structure and Operations of the BND

The organization of the BND was patterned on both Western intelligence agencies and the pre-existing Gehlen Organization, integrating characteristics that represented its unique position in the Cold War. At the leadership was Reinhard Gehlen, who served as its first president and played a major role in defining its operating structure.

Organizational Structure

The BND was organized to guarantee efficiency and operational effectiveness. It was organized into many important sections, each responsible for distinct parts of intelligence collecting and analysis:

Operations Division: This division was entrusted with executing covert operations, acquiring human intelligence (HUMINT), and coordinating espionage activities. It was responsible for sending operatives, establishing connections, and conducting surveillance both inside Germany and overseas.

Analysis Division: Analysts in this division were responsible for evaluating intelligence reports, creating assessments, and giving strategic insights. This division played a vital role in analyzing the material acquired by the Operations Division and presenting actionable intelligence to policymakers.

Technical Services Division: This division handled the creation and implementation of technology tools and procedures for intelligence collection. It was responsible for electronic surveillance, signal intelligence (SIGINT), and the deployment of cutting-edge technology to assist field operations.

Administrative and Support Division: This division controlled the internal operations of the

BND, including personnel, logistical, and financial problems. It guaranteed that the agency's many tasks worked smoothly and effectively.

Operations and Methodologies

The BND's activities were characterized by a combination of conventional espionage tactics and new intelligence procedures. The agency focuses on several main areas:

Counterintelligence: The BND was responsible for discovering and disarming Soviet and East German intelligence activity inside West Germany. This involves monitoring possible spies, discovering infiltration efforts, and safeguarding critical information.

Political and Military Intelligence: The BND gathered intelligence on Soviet military capabilities, political events in Eastern Bloc nations, and strategic intents of Communist leaders. This information was vital for defining West Germany's military plans and contributing to NATO's strategic planning.

Economic and Scientific Intelligence: Understanding the economic and technical capabilities of the Eastern Bloc was crucial for preserving a competitive advantage. The BND acquired information on industrial breakthroughs, scientific achievements, and technical discoveries in Communist nations.

Allied Cooperation: The BND cooperated closely with its Western partners, notably the CIA, MI6, and other NATO intelligence services. This collaboration includes exchanging information, coordinating actions, and supporting cooperative measures to oppose the Soviet threat.

Challenges and Innovations

The BND had significant problems in its early years, including the necessity to construct a new intelligence network from scratch and solve the complexity of Cold War espionage. The agency had to manage the legacy of the Gehlen Organization, integrate previous Nazi intelligence assets, and build credibility within the Western intelligence community.

Innovations in intelligence collecting and analysis were key to the BND's success. The agency embraced sophisticated technology, such as early computer systems for data processing and secure communications techniques, to boost its capabilities. Additionally, the BND earned a reputation for excellent counterintelligence operations, which helped secure West Germany from internal and foreign threats.

Collaboration with Western Intelligence Agencies

The BND's partnership with Western intelligence agencies was a cornerstone of its efficacy and a crucial component in its success throughout the Cold War. This partnership was founded on common interests and the shared purpose of combating Soviet influence.

CIA Cooperation

The collaboration between the BND and the CIA was especially crucial. The BND's early years were defined by strong cooperation with the

CIA, which provided financial backing, technical aid, and strategic direction. This relationship was vital for building the BND's operational capabilities and linking its intelligence operations with wider Western initiatives.

The CIA and BND shared information on a broad variety of matters, including Soviet military activity, political events in Eastern Europe, and technological progress. Joint operations and coordinated activities enabled both agencies to exploit their unique strengths and boost their overall intelligence performance.

NATO Intelligence Sharing

As a member of NATO, West Germany's intelligence contributions were important to the alliance's collective security operations. The

BND engaged in NATO's intelligence-sharing processes, offering crucial insights and evaluations that guided alliance plans and policies. This alliance helped ensure a cohesive strategy for fighting the Soviet threat and sustaining regional peace.

European Intelligence Networks

The BND also cooperated closely with other European intelligence services, notably MI6, the French intelligence agency, and the intelligence services of other NATO member nations. These partnerships permitted information sharing, coordinated actions, and concerted attempts to address similar security challenges.

Joint Operations and Strategic Initiatives

The BND's cooperation with Western intelligence agencies extended to joint operations and strategic objectives.

This comprised coordinated espionage actions, combined counterintelligence efforts, and cooperation research and development initiatives. The cooperation between the BND and its Western allies had a major role in establishing the intelligence environment during the Cold War.

Chapter 8: Espionage in the Cold War

The Cold War, a period of geopolitical tension between the United States and the Soviet Union, ran from the conclusion of World War II to the breakup of the Soviet Union in 1991. Espionage played a vital role throughout this century, with information collecting and covert operations shaping diplomatic relations, military plans, and international politics.

Reinhard Gehlen, having converted from a senior Nazi intelligence officer to a crucial figure in Western intelligence, profoundly affected espionage efforts during this time. This section discusses major operations and intelligence collection initiatives, Gehlen's effect on Cold War dynamics, and his significant achievements and failures.

Key Operations and Intelligence Gathering

The Gehlen Organization

After World War II, Reinhard Gehlen, who had previously been the commander of the Wehrmacht's intelligence on the Eastern Front, was essential in forming what would become known as the Gehlen Organization.

This clandestine intelligence network was first established up in 1946 with the cooperation of the American intelligence organizations, particularly the CIA. The agency was entrusted with collecting information on the Soviet Union and its allies, relying on the massive networks of spies and connections Gehlen had developed throughout the war.

The Gehlen Organization's principal role was to furnish the United States with important intelligence regarding Soviet military capabilities and intentions. Its operatives worked largely in Eastern Europe, acquiring information via a network of former Nazi collaborators, anti-communist partisans, and other individuals with knowledge of Soviet activities.

The Gehlen Organization was exceptionally successful at intercepting and studying Soviet communications and understanding Soviet military plans.

Operation Gold (or Operation Stopwatch)

One of the most prominent operations involving the Gehlen Organization was Operation Gold, a large espionage campaign performed by the CIA and British intelligence. Launched in 1954, this operation comprised the building of a tunnel that connected to Soviet communication connections in Berlin. The Gehlen Organization supplied important intelligence that aided in planning and conducting the operation.

The tunnel, which extended from the British sector of Berlin into the Soviet-controlled region, was meant to intercept and decode Soviet communications.

Although the project was ultimately compromised—discovered by the Soviets who subsequently utilized it for counterintelligence—the information acquired from the tunnel gave vital insights into Soviet military and political strategy.

Operation Wringer

Another significant effort was effort Wringer, which was begun in the late 1950s. This operation intended to infiltrate and disrupt Soviet spy networks operating in Western Europe. The Gehlen Organization played a significant role in discovering and disarming Soviet spies and their networks.

By exploiting its considerable intelligence sources and experience, the group was able to deliver actionable information that led to the arrest and expulsion of many Soviet spies. The operation was part of a wider attempt to thwart Soviet intelligence efforts and prevent Soviet infiltration of Western governments and organizations. It emphasized the Gehlen Organization's success in not just acquiring information but also in combating the operations of opposing intelligence services.

Counterintelligence and Psychological Operations

Beyond typical espionage, the Gehlen Organization was also active in counterintelligence and psychological operations. This includes attempts to influence and destabilize communist governments and promote anti-communist groups.

By using its awareness of Soviet tactics and psychological profiles, the group was able to execute operations that damaged Soviet dominance in numerous places.

These psychological operations were designed to foster dissension among communist states and encourage anti-communist sentiments in targeted countries. The effectiveness of these activities contributed to the wider policy of containment and influence throughout the Cold War.

Gehlen's Impact on Cold War Dynamics

Strengthening Western Intelligence Capabilities

Reinhard Gehlen's shift from a senior Nazi intelligence official to a vital asset of the Western intelligence community had a dramatic influence on Cold War dynamics. His skills and network offered the United States and its allies significant information about Soviet operations, military tactics, and political moves.

The founding of the Gehlen Organization helped Western intelligence services to better grasp the Soviet threat and create more effective measures for fighting it. Gehlen's understanding of Soviet activities and his ability to use his network of connections were essential in defining Western intelligence policies and actions throughout the Cold War.

Influence on Western Military and Political Strategies

The information produced by the Gehlen Organization affected Western military and political policies during the Cold War. Information on Soviet military capabilities and intentions helped define NATO's defensive plans and military preparations. Gehlen's insights into Soviet tactics and plans were utilized to devise responses and improve Western military positions.

Politically, the intelligence obtained by the Gehlen Organization helped to the development of Western policy against the Soviet Union and its allies. The information produced by Gehlen and his group was used to assist diplomatic efforts, negotiate treaties, and formulate tactics for managing international relations throughout the Cold War.

Role in Key Cold War Events

Gehlen's effect on Cold War dynamics was obvious in numerous significant events and crises. His intelligence network played a significant role in the Cuban Missile Crisis of 1962, supplying information on Soviet missile installations in Cuba. This knowledge was vital in developing the Western reaction to the situation and averting a possible nuclear clash.

Additionally, Gehlen's group contributed crucial information throughout other regional conflicts and proxy battles, including those in the Middle East and Southeast Asia. The knowledge acquired helped define Western engagement and strategy in these wars.

Notable Successes and Failures

Successes

One of the significant triumphs of Gehlen's career was the formation and functioning of the Gehlen Organization. The organization's capacity to offer precise and useful information on Soviet actions was a notable accomplishment and helped Western triumphs in the Cold War.

The success of operations such as Operation Gold, despite its final compromise, established the organization's potential for high-level information collecting and analysis. The information collected from the operation gave vital insights into Soviet communications and helped Western knowledge of Soviet military strategy.

Additionally, the counterintelligence measures done by the Gehlen Organization, especially Operation Wringer, were effective in discovering and neutralizing Soviet spy networks. These initiatives helped defend Western interests and prevent Soviet penetration of important institutions.

Failures

Despite these triumphs, Gehlen's career was not without its setbacks and scandals. One major failure was the ultimate compromise of Operation Gold. Although the operation yielded useful information, its discovery by the Soviets resulted in a considerable loss of confidence and a rethinking of espionage procedures.

The Gehlen Organization also faced issues linked to its dependence on former Nazi collaborators and anti-communist partisans. The use of these sources often led to erroneous or biased information, which hindered the success of certain missions.

Furthermore, Gehlen's participation in questionable psychological operations and attempts to undermine communist countries generated ethical and legal questions. These actions, although helpful to Western aims, also led to critiques and discussions regarding the tactics utilized in intelligence operations.

Chapter 9: Controversies and Criticisms

Reinhard Gehlen's post-war career was plagued by continuous suspicions of his Nazi sympathies and complicity in war crimes. As Hitler's Chief of Intelligence on the Eastern Front, Gehlen was directly associated with the Wehrmacht's operations in one of the most brutal theaters of World War II.

His role in orchestrating intelligence and military strategies against the Soviet Union led to significant scrutiny once his name came into the public and intelligence community spotlight. Gehlen's role as the leader of the Fremde Heere Ost (Foreign Armies East) made him a major figure in the Nazi military system. This squad was responsible for obtaining information on Soviet military actions and was inextricably entangled with the horrors perpetrated by the Nazi dictatorship on the Eastern Front. The degree of murder and repression that typified the Eastern Front ultimately connected people in high-ranking positions, including Gehlen, in the greater story of Nazi war crimes.

Critics have maintained that Gehlen's membership in the Nazi military intelligence apparatus could not be disentangled from the regime's larger criminal actions.

The Wehrmacht's intelligence activities frequently assisted or enabled the harsh suppression of partisan opposition and the persecution of civilians, particularly Jews and other targeted groups. Gehlen's techniques and the information he supplied were important to the execution of the Nazi war effort and the implementation of occupation policies that led to innumerable crimes.

Despite his post-war attempts to dissociate himself from the Nazi government, Gehlen's participation in managing actions that led to these crimes remained a major focus of criticism. His role in the intelligence agency throughout the war sparked concerns about his culpability and the ethical consequences of his conduct.

For many historians and critics, the degree to which Gehlen's intelligence efforts were directly related to war crimes remains a disputed subject, casting a lasting shadow over his reputation.

Internal and External Critiques of Gehlen's Methods

Gehlen's transformation from a high-ranking Nazi intelligence officer to a significant figure in Western intelligence operations was not without its hurdles and critiques. Internally, among the intelligence community, Gehlen encountered suspicion and opposition.

Many American and British intelligence personnel were dubious of Gehlen's intentions and techniques. They questioned if his allegiance had actually moved or whether he was merely exploiting his new post to achieve his own goal.

Gehlen's technique also came under attack. His dependence on former Nazi agents and their networks for intelligence collection prompted worries about the veracity and ethical implications of the information he supplied. Critics stated that Gehlen's intelligence activities were compromised by his prior associations and the inherent prejudices of his informants.

The employment of veteran Nazi intelligence operatives and their links, while offering significant insights into Soviet actions, also offered an opportunity for disinformation and manipulation.

Externally, Gehlen received criticism from different sectors, including former wartime rivals and modern critics of Cold War policy. Many considered his change from a Nazi espionage head to a Cold War ally as ethically problematic. His engagement with the CIA and other Western agencies was considered by some as a pragmatic, although problematic, convergence of interests. Critics suggested that Gehlen's role in intelligence operations during the Cold War was a disturbing indication of the propensity of Western powers to disregard previous ties for strategic objectives.

Additionally, Gehlen's approach to intelligence was generally considered as too concentrated on Soviet military capabilities to the detriment of other areas of Soviet culture and politics.

This limited emphasis occasionally led to incorrect evaluations and lost chances to comprehend the full context of Soviet activities. The dependence on Gehlen's intelligence, especially in the early years of the Cold War, was therefore a topic of dispute among intelligence experts and politicians who thought that a more nuanced approach was required.

Gehlen's Responses and Defenses

In reaction to these claims and critiques, Reinhard Gehlen maintained an attitude of defensive reasoning and strategic positioning. Gehlen repeatedly stressed the pragmatic character of his post-war work and attempted to underline the strategic value of his intelligence efforts.

He stated that his move from a Nazi to a Cold War operator was driven by a real desire to oppose the Soviet menace and safeguard democratic ideals, rather than any personal or ideological attachment.

Gehlen's writings and public speeches sometimes contained a justification for his wartime activities. He claimed that his major concentration had always been on successful information collection and military strategy, rather than the political or moral consequences of his work.

Gehlen viewed himself as a devoted professional who responded to changing conditions and who had a vital part in building the post-war intelligence scene.

To rebut the claims of collaboration in war crimes, Gehlen and his followers stated that his position in the Nazi system was entirely professional and did not necessarily represent his ideas or principles. They said that his post-war contributions to Western intelligence were proof of his dedication to democratic values and his readiness to collaborate with erstwhile rivals for the greater good.

In terms of internal criticisms, Gehlen frequently referred to his successful formation of the Bundesnachrichtendienst (BND) and his efficient coordination with Western intelligence organizations as proof of his capacity and dependability. He portrayed his techniques as a necessary response to the growing intelligence demands of the Cold War, suggesting that his skills and network were important assets in the battle against Soviet expansion.

Gehlen's responses also included a larger condemnation of the intelligence community's emphasis on his history rather than his contributions to Cold War security. He stated that the historical background of his activities was being exploited to damage his credibility and effectiveness, rather than being judged in terms of his concrete influence on intelligence and security.

Chapter 10: Retirement and Memoirs

In the fall of 1968, Reinhard Gehlen, having spent decades at the vanguard of intelligence and espionage, formally resigned from his job as the chief of West Germany's Bundesnachrichtendienst (BND). His retirement was a landmark milestone, marking the conclusion of a career that had seen him go from a high-ranking Nazi official to a crucial role in the Western intelligence establishment throughout the Cold War.

By the time Gehlen took down, he had converted the BND from a young intelligence organization into a well-organized and efficient enterprise. His tenure witnessed the formation of a formidable intelligence network that contributed considerably to Western security during a critical age of geopolitical conflict. Gehlen's retirement was not a retreat into obscurity; rather, it signaled a change in his concentration from operational intelligence to reflecting on his amazing life and career.

Despite retiring from active intelligence activity, Gehlen remained a significant figure in the realm of foreign relations and espionage. His thoughts and experiences were sought by many governments, organizations, and academic institutions.

The conclusion of his career heralded the beginning of a new period when he would give unique thoughts on the dynamics of intelligence and its role in world politics.

Publication of His Memoirs

Gehlen's retirement led to the publishing of his memoirs, which gave a rare and extensive account of his experiences. His principal publication, "The Gehlen Memoirs," released in 1971, offers an unmatched view into the mind of one of the 20th century's most prominent spies.

The memoirs were notable not just for their first-hand depiction of espionage operations but also for their insights into the complicated interaction between intelligence and politics.

The publishing of the memoirs was a methodically planned project, demonstrating Gehlen's mastery of storytelling and history. His work was defined by a mix of thorough remembrance and purposeful omission, aiming at both disclosing and safeguarding sensitive material. Gehlen's memoirs did not just describe events but also gave insights into the strategic choices he made and their ramifications for world affairs.

The book was received with tremendous curiosity by historians, political experts, and the general public. It was regarded as an essential addition to the knowledge of intelligence operations and Cold War dynamics.

Gehlen's ability to communicate the nuances of espionage and his role in establishing the intelligence environment was highly acknowledged, making his memoirs an essential resource for anyone researching the period.

Public and Private Reflections on His Career

In the years after his retirement, Gehlen participated in both public and private thoughts on his career. Publicly, he appeared at numerous conferences, seminars, and interviews, where he presented his ideas on intelligence work, espionage, and international relations.

His observations generally addressed the ethical and strategic issues he experienced throughout his career, as well as his opinions on the growth of intelligence methods.

Privately, Gehlen was known to engage in intense contemplation about his background. His exchanges with intimate friends, coworkers, and historians generally provided a more nuanced understanding of his experiences. He focused on the moral implications of his job, the nature of his partnerships, and the influence of his judgments on the larger geopolitical scene. These private thoughts gave a more comprehensive view of Gehlen's motives and the ethical issues underpinning his work.

Contributions to Intelligence and Espionage

Gehlen's contributions to intelligence and espionage were extensive and complex. His work during World War II, notably on the Eastern Front, proved his outstanding talents in information collecting and analysis. He built and maintained a vast network of informants and operations, giving important intelligence that affected military strategy and results.

After the war, Gehlen's influence stretched into the Cold War period, when his role in forming and heading the BND was important. He effectively adapted his wartime intelligence skills to the new setting of Cold War geopolitics, developing a sophisticated intelligence network that played a key role in Western security. His ability to move from a Nazi commander to a recognized intelligence head for the Allies underlined his outstanding flexibility and strategic brilliance.

Gehlen's accomplishments also included the creation of novel intelligence procedures and the strengthening of international intelligence collaboration. His work set the basis for current intelligence procedures and helped the formulation of Western intelligence strategy during a pivotal moment in history.

Long-Term Effects on Cold War Policies
The influence of Gehlen's work on Cold War policy was enormous. His foundation of the

BND and his intelligence efforts profoundly affected Western plans and reactions to Soviet operations. The intelligence given by Gehlen's network helped affect governmental choices, military plans, and diplomatic approaches during the Cold War.

Gehlen's intelligence efforts were essential in understanding Soviet intentions and capabilities, helping Western nations to create better informed and successful strategies. His insights on Soviet military and political objectives helped the establishment of containment policies and defensive measures that were crucial to the Western response to Soviet expansionism.

Moreover, Gehlen's effective integration of former Nazi intelligence assets into the BND highlighted the intricacy and practicality of Cold

War intelligence methods. His ability to use these assets for Western intelligence goals demonstrated the pragmatic attitude employed by Western intelligence organizations during this time.

Historical and Contemporary Views on His Legacy

Gehlen's legacy is regarded through numerous perspectives, both historical and modern. Historically, he is acknowledged as an important player in 20th-century intelligence, whose work had a lasting influence on Cold War dynamics and intelligence operations. His shift from a Nazi commander to a major intelligence figure for the Allies remains a matter of great curiosity and discussion.

Contemporary opinions on Gehlen's legacy are informed by continuous arguments regarding the ethical and political consequences of his work. While he is praised for his services to intelligence and Western security, there is also criticism surrounding his former ties and the ethical implications of his work.

Contemporary historians and commentators continue to study the complexity of his career, balancing his successes with the wider context of his activities throughout the conflict.

Overall, Gehlen's legacy is a monument to his outstanding talents and agility as a spy, as well as a reflection of the sophisticated and sometimes ethically ambiguous world of intelligence. His career remains a topic of study and conversation, giving significant insights into the nexus of espionage, politics, and history.

Conclusion

Reinhard Gehlen's career is a study in contrasts, typified by his transformation from a high-ranking Nazi intelligence officer to a significant participant in the American and West German intelligence organizations.

His biography reflects a curious duality: on one side, he was a key person in the Third Reich's military intelligence organization; on the other, he became a crucial asset in creating the intelligence landscape of the post-war world. This contradiction not only underlines the depth of his character but also illustrates the delicate interaction between historical circumstances and human agency.

Nazi Intelligence Officer:

Gehlen's service as Hitler's senior intelligence officer on the Eastern Front was defined by a combination of strategic genius and merciless practicality. Appointed by Heinz Guderian, Gehlen was charged with managing the Wehrmacht's intelligence efforts against the Soviet Union.

His efforts led to the formation of a very successful network of spies and informants, which gave important knowledge about Soviet army movements, plans, and capabilities. Gehlen's system was remarkable for its breadth of coverage and the trustworthiness of its intelligence, which frequently provided the Wehrmacht a tactical advantage on the Eastern Front.

Despite the crucial significance of his work, Gehlen's tenure in the Nazi dictatorship was not without criticism. His relationship with the Third Reich and his participation in the greater Nazi war effort garnered intense examination.

The techniques deployed by his intelligence network, including the use of force and deceit, were by the cruel tactics of the government, leaving a legacy that was as ethically problematic as it was tactically efficient.

American and West German Intelligence Leader:

The conclusion of World War II witnessed Gehlen's sudden change from a senior Nazi agent to a critical friend of the United States. As the Third Reich disintegrated, Gehlen perceived an opportunity to shift from a fallen dictatorship to a new position as an informant for the Allies. His supply of knowledge on the Soviet Union, along with his wide network of former Nazi agents, made him a significant asset to the American intelligence agency.

Under Operation Paperclip, Gehlen's shift was assisted, enabling him to dodge possible punishment and instead exploit his expertise and relationships to aid the United States. His work with the CIA was essential in defining American intelligence tactics throughout the early Cold War years.

Gehlen's formation of the Gehlen Organization, which subsequently developed into the Bundesnachrichtendienst (BND), was a remarkable success. His efforts helped to develop a comprehensive intelligence architecture that played a crucial part in West Germany's security and its contributions to Western intelligence activities.

Gehlen's post-war career was marked by his strategic brilliance and his ability to manage the difficult political terrain of the Cold War. His remarkable transition from a former Nazi intelligence head to a significant role in the Western intelligence community underlines his flexibility and the pragmatism of his approach to intelligence work.

It also underscores the contentious aspect of his legacy, since his former associations were sometimes overlooked by his services to Western security.

Final Thoughts on His Place in History

Reinhard Gehlen has a unique and problematic role in history. His career reflects the intricacies and moral difficulties of the 20th century's most chaotic moments. As an intelligence officer for Nazi Germany, Gehlen was closely engaged in the strategic operations of a dictatorship that was responsible for immense crimes.

His role in helping the war effort and obtaining important information against the Soviet Union was essential, but it was also enmeshed with the greater moral and ethical difficulties involved with the Nazi system.

The move from Nazi intelligence head to American ally is undoubtedly the most remarkable part of Gehlen's career. It highlights the frequently pragmatic and opportunistic character of post-war geopolitics. Gehlen's ability to deliver important information and sustain operational efficiency made him a desirable asset to the United States, despite his prior associations. This element of his work emphasizes the realpolitik that frequently defines international interactions, where strategic rewards may occasionally eclipse moral concerns.

Gehlen's significance in the Cold War period cannot be understated. The Gehlen Organization and its successor, the BND, were essential in developing Western intelligence activities and resisting Soviet influence. Gehlen's experience in Soviet military strategy and his ability to negotiate complicated intelligence operations offered the Western allies important advantages during a moment of heightened tension and uncertainty. His services contributed to ensuring West Germany's status in the Western bloc and assisted the larger aims of NATO and the United States in the Cold War.

However, Gehlen's legacy is also marred by criticism. His involvement with the Nazi government and the techniques adopted during his stint as a Nazi intelligence official has put a lengthy shadow over his post-war accomplishments.

The ethical implications of his transfer and the employment of former Nazi personnel in post-war intelligence activities have been issues of serious controversy. Gehlen's career highlights the difficulty of reconciling previous deeds with new duties in a changing global order.

In appraising Gehlen's position in history, it is vital to consider both his accomplishments and his problematic background. His career highlights the delicate dynamics of intelligence work and the frequently confusing nature of historical legacies.

Gehlen's narrative is a reminder of the multidimensional character of historical people, whose acts may have far-reaching implications that transcend their local circumstances.

Ultimately, Reinhard Gehlen's double existence epitomizes the tensions and ambiguities of the 20th century. His transition from a Nazi intelligence officer to a pivotal role in Cold War intelligence shows the complicated interaction between morality, strategy, and historical circumstance. As history continues to reflect on Gehlen's life and career, it is necessary to analyze both the strategic significance of his work and the ethical implications of his acts. In doing so, we acquire a clearer picture of the man behind the intelligence operations and the wider dynamics that formed his incredible career.

www.ingramcontent.com/pod-product-compliance
Lightning Source LLC
Chambersburg PA
CBHW071932210526
45479CB00002B/643